TRAWLERMAN'S TURQUOISE

Matthew Caley's *Thirst* (Slow Dancer, 1999) was shortlisted for the Forward Prize for Best First Collection. He's published five more since, three with Bloodaxe, *Apparently* (2010), *Rake* (2016), and *Trawlerman's Turquoise* (2019), his sixth. His work has featured in many anthologies including *Poems of the Decade* (Forward Worldwide, 2011), *Identity Parade: New British and Irish Poetry* (Bloodaxe Books, 2010) and *The Picador Book of Love Poems* (Picador, 2011). He's read his work from Morden Tower, Newcastle, to the National Portrait Gallery, London; from Galway to Novi Sad. In previous lives he was on the fringe of the Small Press revival in the 1980s; designed record sleeves; lived in squats in Brixton during the 80s–90s; and has taught in art schools. Recently, he's tutored for the Poetry School and taught Contemporary Poetry/Creative Writing at the School of English, University of St Andrews. He lives in London with the Czech artist Pavla Alchin and their two daughters, Iris and Mina.

MATTHEW CALEY

Trawlerman's Turquoise

BLOODAXE BOOKS

Copyright © Matthew Caley 2019

ISBN: 978 1 78037 488 8

First published 2019 by
Bloodaxe Books Ltd
Eastburn
South Park
Hexham
Northumberland NE46 1BS

www.bloodaxebooks.com
For further information about Bloodaxe titles
please visit our website and join our mailing list
or write to the above address for a catalogue.

 Supported using public funding by
**ARTS COUNCIL
ENGLAND**

Cover design by Neil Astley, Pamela Robertson-Pearce,
Pavla Alchin & Matthew Caley.

Printed in Great Britain by Bell & Bain Limited, Glasgow, Scotland, on
acid-free paper sourced from mills with FSC chain of custody certification.

for Pavla, Iris and Mina as always
and i.m. Robert Growka

[and for all my enemies –
if only I could remember who you are]

ACKNOWLEDGEMENTS

are due to the editors of the following magazines, journals, anthologies and websites where these poems, or versions of them, were first published: *Magma Poetry,* www.morningstar.co.uk, *New Boots and Pantisocracies* blogspot, *Poetry London, The Poetry Review*; one stanza of '*from* The Foldings' was published in *Lookout: Poems from Aldeburgh Beach* (Lookout Editions, 2016, ed. Tamar Yoseloff); several more stanzas were featured in *Tentacular www.tentacularmag.com.* 'Slow Blow Job' was originally written for the event *Metamorphic Rock: Poets take over the Chelsea Hotel* (with Bob Gruen's Rock Seen exhibition) organised by Jon Stone; '[Prayer for] The Frazzled' was irresponsibly slipped out like a silverfish into an ordinary Facebook post. 'Thaw', 'Epistolary Novels', 'Line-Lengths' and 'Basilisk' were read as part of a collaboration with poet Cheryl Moskowitz and musicians Ian Burdge and Alastair Gavin in the *All Saints Sessions* series.

Thanks to Tiffany Atkinson – with love and theft – for a phrase included in 'from The Foldings'. To Melissa Lee-Houghton for insightful correspondence.

'The Truce' owes everything to *Skřivánci na niti (Larks on a String)* [dir. Jiří Menzel, 1969] based on a book by Bohumil Hrabal. 'The Waterfall' is dedicated to Peter Perrett, but not necessarily about him.

I would like to thank the Royal Literary Fund and the Society of Authors for grants that helped during the writing of this book. All the grand people at the Poetry School, London, and the School of English at the University of St Andrews; to Neil and Pamela for Romanian Embassy invites and much else besides.

As always, a huge "all hail" to Mr Andy Ching for his ear and eye.

CONTENTS

poets tend to incarnate by the side of ocean, at least in vision, if inland far they be. Or if some blocking agent excludes any glimpse of that immortal sea, various surrogates readily enough are found

HAROLD BLOOM, *A Map of Misreading*

I am become
dumb
in answer
to your dead language of amor

MINA LOY, 'Letters of the Un-living'

Yeats tried another tactic. Sitting at a table with his long arm stretched out before him, he bent down to try to communicate through telepathy. Suddenly his arm began to tremble and throb as if under the influence of the machine, which gratifyingly appeared to obey commands to stop and start. But no more words emerged.

BRENDA MADDOX, *Yeats's Ghosts: The Secret Life of W.B. Yeats*

But it seems to me that the effects of, the products of, human intelligence, are almost biological functions, you know, like the urine of dogs that's full of information for other dogs. There is an almost excremental, in the most innocent and noble sense, aspect to what we do, to our "droppings".

JAMES MERRILL, from *Twentieth-Century Literature*
(Winter 1992), interview by C.A. Buckley

I've come to realise that Graves is right, that The Muse has to be female – the feminine principle is the source...

THOM GUNN, *London Magazine* (December 1977)
interview by W.I. Scobie

The Vltava

by a drain cover
by a bay tree   Turner Street
something is in spate
– The Creole Girl, inhaling –
one lean underground river
seeks similar for meet   or

slivers it out there
taps an *Uber* cab – twisting through MittelEurope
as fast as a man can type

Thaw

I

as the Vltava
thaws into spick rivulets
puce onion domes
the iron clang of snowdrops
drip-drop   glub of spawning pike

as a waist-high spate
runs hard into the Effra
under a culvert
as our blood mingles
in the pale, petulant child

her shrug of duvet
gamelan of slant harebells
played by Léon Theremin

retrograde in Petrograd
don't touch this Ether-phone but
trace the aura of your hair

past crayfish in cress
past eighteen types of orchids
the river taxis to where

II

floodwater meets thighs
fauve-scum tidemark garters pinch
thin film of stocking
rippling back – Foley artists
rubbing up rougher stockings

these meander-scars
ne meander-scar or scarp
make an oxbow lake
crescentic cut in the bluff
drying or dried meander

queues merge and re-group
thin tape of river between
serried birches – wetted banks

bloodstream of borders
the passport's baby photo
compared to an eight-year-old

who owns your forehead's
telltale heirloom nose wrinkle
the border guard bends to check

III
airport body-scans
a searching uniform face
tracing up your legs
between your knees making A
– fillings   coins   panic music –

you're a tuning fork
that piercing ping at the crux
denim stud-button
then you become a pylon
two frisk your pinkish aura

as sunset on steel
those Chinese ideograms
with triangular meanings

undress the evening
your spine knots so exposed are
pebbles on a riverbed

the unsaid solid
as the unsaid always is
so solid and one-sided

IV
take a sharp corner
merge with the Elbe at Mêlník
garlic   slivovitz
Smetana's six symphonic
poems crackling with static

which, withdrawn, will leave
frequency oscillators
a lacy-foam hem
and the thigh of a stream-sylph
steaming like Turkish coffee

as stress leaves your face
all of these hurts will migrate
riverbanks' dirt-green gamboge

vibrating bridges
tremble under Robert Moog –
loose your rain-loosened girdle

trace the outline of
a horse from nose-band to butt
then into the Vltava

Stendhal Syndrome

as when Stendhal swooned
in the vast basilica
floating up the dome
like a loosed weather balloon,
to dislodge a tiny glyph
of mica from a
mosaic. It blinks now from
this Shadwell pavement
as a snail-trail down a kerb
by this part-torn *Tesco* bag.

glyph off an aged
fresco! – wink in bitumen
so everyone feints at the

dull everyday,
as women in taut corsets
would faint in front of paintings

In Praise of Turkish Coffee

three sisters stand on
a balcony, mid–
winter, their laughter steam but
the balcony latticework
   mist, ripped *Camel* packets, they

   play *Chemin de Fer*
or sip at Turkish coffee.
Two men. A factory roof –
fingers or mittens?
   mittens / fingers. An oil drum

   another oil drum.
Two aerials sway.
Radio mast. One man, bald,
to the left, who coughs, will wait
   for his Turkish coffee. One

   father, a tree to
his climbing daughters who jump,
smother him, he lists
a little unsteadily,
   laughs post-scuffle, spills Turkish

   coffee. Five on an
opposite roof, egg white sky
smoking, barter bread
and hummus, discuss some blast
   that has or has not gone off,

   as ibriks simmer–
shimmer. Whiskers-in-the-air
cat on the guard rail.
One tall man – an ectomorph –
   a fig-tree, woman tying

her garter, gold-hued,
bending from the waist seen through
a grilled window, a
dwarf, half-pissed [say, quarter-pissed?]
   in need of Turkish coffee.

*   Frank O'Hara once*
praised instant coffee
but a better man might have
kept shtum. A worse sense
   of Western taste was rarely

   committed to print
he missed out greatly by not
praising Turkish grains.
But back to that balcony,
   more hole now than tracery

   where someone stood for
something once, then something else,
some conspiracy
of this radial palm's ro-
   tating blades of half-green or

   cool-shade filigree
where we sit and won't desist
   from drinking Turkish coffee.

5.00 a.m.

(after Hugo)

tomorrow, at the very instant the entire countryside goes white as
    phosphor,
I will be off. Knowing you are resigned
to wait out my arrival
I'll wade slowly through fern, traipse painfully over fell
even though we have been too long apart.
I'll keep an eye on my thoughts as I walk – see nothing [hood down],
hear nothing [earphones in], solo, not known,
bent double, hands folded, down, the white nights and black nights

    fused so I don't see flush evening fall
nor that bleached yacht
headed for harbour. Once there, I'll place a circuit

    of cinquefoil on your sepulchre,
followed by
a spray of sweet thorn.

Epistolary Novels

I

supposedly my
eyes see only violet
– the one true colour –
though this window has no blind
I see a violet blind
so up comes that blind
behind it   another blind
so I pull that up
behind it a violet sill
on that a vase of violets

whose sepals display
a Pantone shade of   dolour
we are in a bind
epistolary novels
stacked high on the sill behind

II

epistolary
epistolary novels!
epistolary
novels in the email age
the ether alive with them
all our unsaid thoughts
epistolary novels
scratched out, never mailed
workmen put down your shovels!
epistolary novels

I wrote a letter
about epistolary
novels, several
in fact, they would make a book
it raised my serotonin

III

    levels   Well known fact:
raised serotonin levels
make you see violet
and is that not only an
n away from violent?
as a slant blind look
at a rectangle of light
makes of our eyes – rectangles!
then violet frills at the wrist
that block our entire outlook

    we are galley slaves, my sweet
co-sanguine and coeval
hot rebuffing cold
low on the sill of your breast
an earlobe thaws on a heart

    bow to your betters!
letters beget   more letters
epistolary novels

Aloes Démaquillant

I

chill   chill-white   chill tiles
chill bathroom gone green with spring
security glass
obscuring the sight
of *Aloes Démaquillant*
slow-filling with gob-green light
– windows' frogspawn bubble wrap
balms, eye drops, ointments –
then *Aloes Démaquillant*
Balm of Gilead
deep in the porous membrane
tragedy   a Greek chorus

II

you bathe with quiver
angled across your bare back
to keep the feathers
dry   stay the arrow's true flight
I'm a buck   the hounds gaining
grey buffering sun
blister packs   disappointment
gels *Gumption* and grout
a world gone pixelated –
lasso'd by a fauve scum-line

give me what I want
[or certainly need, a bath]   *grain*   the city at evening
sky-dome Fullerene
give me what I want   your skin
and *Aloes Démaquillant*

Summoning Spell

   for sheer need of you
I tried a summoning spell
[apprentice-magician]
the syllables of your name
– two, three? – held over naked flame
which soon gave off gas
a yellow petal inside
a half-mauve petal
purple rim   twisted, over-
lapping and writhing

   asterisks flooded
then into a password box
a file clicked open
ice-crust formed on a gall oak
third on the left in this park

   ice-melt in the give
of your back   no avail   so
much for the summoning spell

Telepathy

I

by telepathy
lure them all to the lighthouse
tactile as sound is
that gamelan of rain drips
the underground Ravensbourne
heard through a grating
Buckminster Fuller's
terrible migraine
thinks the Millennium Dome
a breast's slight curvature as

seen from the left side
and slightly behind   the curve
– one thousand light years –
blithe away an hour   pylons
bowed undertow of cables

II

I bought them through air,
moths in a night-lamp   under-
lit trees   mute sirens
a green phosphorescent park
railings   a single lost glove
the slow-moving cable cars
tuned to a struck gamelan
pond fly tiptoe on algae
rain in a   spacesuit
pine-cinder   fire in the firs
where sound is the tactile sense

two fingers   goodbye
a surge through hand-linked pylons
like binary code
where no one is   *Solaris*
man and wife and   gravity

III
    inappropriate
touch in the mind   is just that
inappropriate
touching   hidden certainty
a kneecap as satellite
isobars simmer
in a weatherman's jacket
in 405 lines
slowed cars on a flyover
score an orchestral soundtrack

    imaginary
wife; imaginary love-
er; floating couple
who crowd-surf the furniture
always   missing each other

Bay Tree on Turner Street

you're gone, Green Afro,
freed from your ankle-bracelet.
Whenever we gaze
into space [always] it's at
the exact height of your eyes –

grey–green? three or two?
monumental steel and glass
which blink, glance back, glazed.
Aerials fraying a roof,
mercury on a hotplate

by *Donatellos*
where street cleaners used to bow
to your frazzled head
amazed. HAND CAR WASH sign   [*tick*]
bored municipal bin   [*tick*]

my dear Green Afro,
swollen head, dysmorphic bole,
feet sunk in concrete,
expand the metropolis
both ways, by being so thin,

convert CO_2
self-medicate with diesel-
fume and chlorophyll.
Your head a geodesic
dome, Fuller's topiary,

an aviary
of back-firing exhausts, spent
we're exhausted from
wanting you – sheer camisole
overhead, tan pantyhose,

taking secateurs
to sky. Green Afro, your clipped
leaves still flavour the pavement

from Aphid Soliloquies

I

myopia is
a little white platelet
sky a drone of glass
we carry no Ether-phones
we tell the time by launderettes
duck the sensor arc
cargo pants sing with coins   keys
sage words   an earache
some watcher will part white noise
like parting a blind   then say

goodbye, Green Afro
this nation's symbol   no oak
but a sapling sleeved in mesh

its stripped off stocking
on the sink estate   nitrous-
oxide cylinders   spit, spit   no growbag

II

today, Green Afro
that rubber belt at your waist
trunk in a frenzy
the wind got inside your head
a head all tug and frazzle
light on the over-
side of leaf   the underside
as if two separate shades
yet they are the same   thrown light
dapples digital billboards

crane reflections   fleet
ivy   a liquid ivy
up sheer sides of glass

you still keep quiet
yet ruck in your rubber belt
one leg in your mesh culotte

The Crossing

Louis Zukofsky
lean-shanked, slow, flips a fag butt
into the Hudson
one more river-sparkle
to douse as a drowned mayfly
amongst the many
catch on an oil slick or
join this torch procession
sinuous from source to mouth
that, sluggish, heads on

via chaos theory
to where our patient huddle
expects it any minute through a sluice pipe by

this dank culvert in Lambeth –
stoic red microdot still
issuing smoke to the sky

Don't Touch that Heater

I could have been enslaved
to the need for her body after all.

THOMAS MERTON

I

lights driven from spring
as if from the century
here, a hotel chair
there   prayer as armour   somewhere
a monk robed in lightning   then:

II

there is a grain of sand in Lambeth
Thomas Merton could not find
a sand grain in the ear
          of skateboarders falling off skateboards   by Chantry Road
          a grain of *Tuinal* in Lambeth
that Satan distributes
          while the daughters of Southwark
          carry their violins by the slurping waters
fennel struggles up out of damp allotments
percolators *shoosh*
          in the little arcades
Styrex cups thrown out   tossed out into the water
    where Satan cannot find a grain of sand
only knotted condoms in drains
              on New Year's morning
          the sky blue as *Tuinal*

there is a grain of sand in the long hall
of the Effra Social
an elm tree drinking the evening
              so its shadow grows light green
                    even on nights

that 21st Century
classic — an oval
face lit up by mobile glow
under an Overground arch —
the new chiaroscuro

there is somewhere Blake's tree in Lambeth
a certain psychogeographer cannot find
there is a pebble of Palestine in Sydenham
           also Sunnis and Shiites over from Afghanistan
                     by the Polski Sklep

there is a grain of fear in the mosques
children holding their father's pillows
to stop themselves flying   or growing up
           because the river is dotted with doused fireflies
                     either side of container barges
                 that only sometimes contain

     such is our largesse, Marge
     there is a grain of sand in Lambeth
academics cannot find
deep in the inner ear
where a voice is at prayer   and, as yet, no answers

III

one gleam left in the sink
as I draw the large curtain
a river turning gilt
in the shitty light   notes on cargo cults
the Ranters outsource injury and insult
     — the point is not to think —
the river lowers   revealed alluvial silts
     — the point is not to be certain —

one fan on the blink
a limbo dancer's navel filling
           with salt
somewhere chefs shucking Moebius strips of melon rind

only one result
when I plug myself into the mains
the networks go monk   pure monk

> *Hector, the Uruguayan*
> *cleaner, on the minimum*
> *wage, his full-on smile*
> *an entire sun – not here.*
> > *The hoovering is begun.*

IV

Here   breath in pure air
The Geography of Lograire
specific   unspecific   OK, everywhere
women dye their hair   with lime
as if there were time   as if they were here

V

You find me in the embrace of a five-foot-long heating fan,
in Abraham's bosom, beyond pain
possibly, eyes blue-red, with a scorch mark down
one side, almost all the way to the groin.

Training at Altitude

admit it, lightweight
that entrance somewhat stunned you
severe portico
from which you get no answer
as tall as Lyle Lovett
maybe as beautiful   [would she like that? what?]
severe and chill and   unusual eyes level
cool as a *Quaalude*   we [both] train at altitude   somewhere inside her
somewhat tacit / illicit
            teasing semi-smile
         'List your many addictions.'
'Recite! Anything,' says she
somewhat lion-coloured   grey-
steel eyes   lynx-like   Sphinx-like   O spare me these
               details!
noted [not correct]
somewhat   necessarily

      somehow she jumbled
the *he* in me and the *she*
in me   with her *he/she* her

      Peroni bottles, iced

so I say a Baudelaire
      'O Thank you,' says she, severe
sincere?   appreciation
'You'd Sleep with Anyone at All, You ------', that one   untoward
Richard Howard here
      being the translator   bare

      Lyle Lovett-tall
carcinogenic as an architect
clear?
much as a tall, iced coffee

31

I am not allowed
to sip   the tops of trees   hair
                stunned by the sheer fact
I can even still be stunned
un-sobriety runs clear

        tell Dis and Demeter to
shove it   go make ready there   some kind of contract
retreat   go   get out   easier, evening air

The Pub Crawl [Slight Return]

I

so, consider my beer glass –
already absorbed
by what is froth and what is body
then leave it on the rickety, wrought iron table
in this dappled beer garden
[deceptive as it opens onto
the bitch and brawl of the inner-city]
– still   frothing   honeyed –
replete with one lime leaf dropped
into its ellipse
from the overhanging, full
and nearly ignited lime trees
through which we might see
the rim of the moon's eclipse,
[heralded blood-red moon] but
everyone here is in their cups
and swaying worse than this table
in the night. I go for a piss.

II

allegedly, the
River Meander was son
to Ocean by way of his sister,
the goddess Thetis, Thetis
– the same – of the sea's riches
and guardian of the world's widest waterways;
Meander, the sort of son who would float out to sea
– see, he *has* issues – let's say quite reluctantly
by going hither and thither
so as to defer the end
[the *end* enclosed in his name]
by refusing to merge with
his father the Ocean,

33

to merge with his mother
the cool, in-brooding, unsung sea
deferring the moment with
each sly swerve and counter-swerve
not to be sea-surge,
not to be pixels in any dispersing aerosol,
nor salt on the yuccas
or any floating vapour, inanimate mineral.
Only to defer, indefinitely

III

    fresh, unfamiliar pain
had, for one instant, over-
lain the startling fact that
an older, familiar
pain had gone, over
this paracetamol then
30mg codeine
and under that – the love-hurt.

IV

    by the triple porcelain – cool, straining, cooling –
between two men
considering, by hint, the angle of our own sway
– and nary a sideways squint –
we three let through us all
that is whey-thin, golden, full,
brothers in relief, and find
in graffiti and piss-scent
the tired and the innocent
stranded in a field of corn.

V

I no longer know
what is froth and what is body
I need water   and a
and a   sinecure   a Sufi
Persephone as a bas–relief

the lime leaf is still
in my beer glass, taut, forlorn,
frothing momentarily
a raft on the Meander.
I sip and we drift from here.

The Level

   writing to deadline
Honoré de Balzac hears
black horses gallop
dips his pen in caffeine downs
fifty-six cups to
formally kick-start the day
coffee black as a hearse is
best on an empty stomach
the vanishing man
he cannot wake up or sleep

   a novel   a play
– his heart will percolate clay –
a play and then a novel

   black horses gallop
cup after tremor-wracked cup
until he finds the level

from **The Foldings**

   Kung walks in a grove
of horizontal cedars
his daemon quietened
those cedars so sideways-on
they seem more horizontal
than their own shadows,
multitudinous voices
rustling in his ear.
Hai-Far holds her blouse straight up
to carry out the silkworms

   cradling the wind
even as it cradles her.
And I would be a
worm in her lap if she would
but feed me one mulberry.

   and the voices say:
'Finding *Rohypnol* in your
post-workout smoothie
is almost like transcendence
...or something.' Then 'Remind me
of Colin's last name.
No? Oh, well I will just call
him Colin.' Six geese
flying in strict formation.
'Your call is valuable

   to us. Don't hang up.'
The rustle of these voices
as if unbidden
like silk. Kung bends to pick up
wayside quatrefoil clovers.

*   *   *

if Mr Bloom found
'the aura of election'
in the hair of a
feminist professor de-
fending any position
so this Poundian
applying his 'non-chrono-
logical notion
of time' finds the word 'email'
in a Troubadour *canzone*.

as rivers might freeze
but only in partial pose,
under ice they seethe
crenulations of the rose,
meltwater, then 'the ocean'.

*   *   *

the fishermen brawl
– pirates, punch-drunks, poetasters –
sneaking their lines out
– striped jerseys! gloss Sou'westers! –
can have but the slightest grip
on this green, climbing tendril
with its motherlode of grapes
kelp and ice splinters
that is one enormous wave

its domed under-curl
has them seasick on dry land
– Melville's cape! – irregular
fumaroles of sloshing foam
surpassing its lace trellis.

*   *   *

'authority wanes –
a good thing'; the stream gravel
speckles the sly trout.
'Authority wanes – a bad
thing'; the sly trout's shadow throws
speckles onto the
gravel. Anyhow,
flows the debate, late and un-
answered by every slant
and meander cutting in-

to the river bank,
tributary after trib-
utary, striped all-
uvial layers, wetted
cinquefoil, coriander.

'my advantage,' he
said 'is surprise', giving it
up in that instant
whilst the kingfisher's dive is
all instance, the dive and the
catch simultaneous and
only the tuning fork of
the alder branch it's after-
math. Only the slightest tear
shows on the river's surface,

the hush–hush toxic
as the tree frog's stippled back.
The agitprop of
flying ants, mica chip on
mica chip – then, the thunder.

'my advantage' he
repeated, redundantly
in the boredom of
the following instant 'is
sup------'. 'Surprise!' we all chorus,
his colonial jacket's
underarm stains in the shape
of annexed islands.
'So, you're ahead of me.' Boom,
Boom the thunder mutters Boom

   lightning and sea-flash
treadmill of opaque turquoise
chrome-brown undertow
of kelp banks. 'History...' he
starts...the thunder interrupts.

*   *   *

   'Fukiyama called
the end of history but
Shirley Bassey called
it right "History repeat-
ing"...on *iPod* shuffle for
eternity. 'And they say
Po-Mo is dead!' The voices
are in overdrive.
'Security cameras
triggered by a blink

   miss everything they
see.' 'No one is criminal
who can get away with it.'
Dust outlines where stood white goods.
'Get that. Shirley got it right.'

*   *   *

supposedly here's
one of those great cedars that seem
what with their wafer-
thin, sideways on, flat-leaf branch
patterns, as a slate-blue shelf
or Erich Heckel's
hands, horizontal
as vertical, a clear smudge
of resinous green
in their shadow opposites,

  someone with their palms
out and downward, lowering,
as if gesturing
to take the pressure off or
lower the temperature. *Chill.*

  we hear from the old
country of how the shadow
of a great tree fell
on a man, just as the great
man's own slant shadow before had
fallen, briefly on
the side of the tree, like light.
How long they lay there
perfectly in unison.
I have now reserved some time

  under this cedar's
still, blue-green horizontals
to lie back and pick
which sharp greeny-blue needles
to pluck from its shadow flats.

*   *   *

if one more poet
compares yonis to figs, or
some vegetable,
again, to the male part, as,
as if that makes them unique
he will puke – sex is
sex, vegetables veget-
ables, neither is Art. Time
to consider the sky: first
slate, then turquoise, now rust red,

exiled as Kung is
with his mate Old Ez who'd give
anything for a
fig, for a fig arbour, for
the sweetest yoni – shit, fig.

*   *   *

'to see is to miss
most things,' says the stately Kung
walking the east wall
'this point cannot compete with
the peripheral at all.'
And a kingfisher,
hearing that, pointed its beak
at the smooth water
wherein lay its diluted
colours. It dived and spread them.

kingfisher's entry
– centrifugal petrol-sheen –
spreading wide outward, branch as catapult
or branch as divining rod.
And all Kung's students miss it.

*   *   *

and the dust rising
gravel-crackle like static
under hoof or foot
– what, centaurs? – sunlight hits on
mint-green of the leaf and the
sure-footed, sorrel horses
melts ideograms
on the Via Rapallo
the slant editor's eyeshade
makes the bay a jade ellipse

so contrapuntal –
'when you come your face scrunches
up like a basil-
isk', post-coital cigarettes
green mint and sorrel horses

the muezzin's song
as counterpoint harmony
to police sirens
the length of Commercial Road
where the sorrel horses sing
the trees into leaf
mint leaf and shade in Shadwell
and the street cleaners
in yellow security
vests texting *Paddy Power*

and a crafty fag
Muslim schoolgirls go hunting
for liquorice lace-
s and *Ka* pineapple pop
sorrel horses nose green mint

*   *   *

'so, 'ice cool' fly boy,
of your magisterial
trouser snake, what gives?'
Such ballast, yet *soi-distant*,
Cynth's glimpse splits you like pack ice.
Though pink yard-lengths of daring
will carry a line
so far, an enjambment can
be painful, require
splints. Wince for your lost mojo.

   as Derrida says
'pen' and 'penis' are from the
same root. The page is
seeded from a virginal
blank by ink. It's seminal.

*   *   *

   'spurn me, spurn me, spurn
me,' she cries, mock-acidly
in the chill bathroom
taking his nipple between
finger and thumb, turning it
like a thermostat.
It's hot. Security glass
and mulled steam, stippled.
He takes an electric tooth-
brush, presses the back of its

   head against her mound.
'Bastard!' she grins, wired
to the burr of thin cotton.
Friends wait on Turkish coffee
in the lounge. Thermostat-hum.

*   *   *

and the voices say:
'Name the Young Hegelians!
– all of them.' They say
'Black boxes are actual-
ly orange.' 'The nurse brought back
an axe from Broadstairs.'
And the winds say: 'From up here
trees are broccoli
florets.' 'My corrupted screen
spins a grey buffering sun.'

    and the voices say:
'Blake's tree in Lambeth
was actually a Bonsai.'
'We are trying to draw e-
mojis for schadenfreude.'

*   *   *

The moth

    'tenderness, yes
for the abandoned mistress
as much as the sweet,
soon-reconciled wife,
much more for each, having both,
abandoning one. Maybe not either, between.'
    As Kung thought this
a silk-moth rose from the wall
fluttering with abandon,
as a wind-blown leaf

    on wind that cooled the wall
as desire cools. *'O yes,*
tenderness born from deceit
is tenderness doubled' he said to the night.
But the moth kept its council.

*   *   *

ilex trees shimmer.
No pig a potentate if
mud holes are legion,
bleached ribs, spars of the beached ship
blind as infatuation.
He draws the ghosted
bra strap across her recline-
ing back, erases
her airport novel. 'Get off'
her given mantra, 'no'

her best compromise.
One microchip lights her arm-
pit in lieu of a
smile. Who is serene, composed.
He himself is the beached ship.

voices so unkind:
'If pigs have the mind of a
three-year-old, then Circe im-
proved men's minds,' they will
whisper beside her ingle.
'Some subjects seem more suited
to drugging.' Ilex trees line
the via negativa.
Kung, high in his mind,

can escape any island.
Even now his nostrils catch
salt-tack tang off the
sea coast, salt tack that causes
the ilex trees to shimmer.

*   *   *

take this sealed, scented
"letter of introduction"
to the fey, sprinting Hai-Far
glimpsed from the 122 bus
– 'extreme wardrobe malfunction' –
some holy unction
from the blue bolt of the sky
without sanction an
– 'extreme wardrobe malfunction' –
rucked tutu and mauve array

CCTV eye
nest of the fly house martin
soft as her soft breast
Coke-wheened scatterlings high five
play bi to get the right guy

smug civic function
MPs geeks and ombudsmen
debate public art
'extreme wardrobe mal...' where the
vol-au-vents lack distinction.
If 'form is function'
then function is shot –
a shot house martin dive-bombs
'extreme wardrobe malfunction'
That 'mal' puts us in mind of

Walter Benjamin's
Art in the Age of Mechan-
ical Reproduc-
tion, 7 [new and used] reviews
– 'extreme wardrobe malfunction' –

    faux décolletage
scooped plump in a bustier
white laced and fraying
'extreme wardrobe malfunction'
cleavage as an illusion
Blu-ray porn vids miss
such louche beauty
of disarray and
ruction – Charlie B's "passing
stranger" [His italics]. Done.

    'extreme wardrobe malfunction'
the scented letters
courtesans don't hide
in their deep scalloped bosoms
the press of such pure fiction

    sink plunge sucker–cup
the sweet pap swelling
[after *deconstruction* they
found it could nourish a child!]
cleavage as illusion
nipple as discourse
house martins, bling, CGI
for this frayed bra strap
– 'extreme wardrobe malfunction' –
Kung will ping in chafed release

    one nipple as star
hackneyed male desire – blah, blah –
Hai-Far aniseed flower
own the means of [re]production
'extreme wardrobe malfunction'

*   *   *

      beach your ship   go to
the gyres of Persephone
beach your ship   go to
the House of Hades
to consult with Tiresias
hide the way from whence
you came   a snail's meander
in dew   uncompressed
swelled and bellying canvas
like a daughter-in-waiting

      hide benevolence
ornament Aphrodite
weigh her down with copper coin
'addressing shades is retro
retro as tupping Circe'

      chorus your readers
these pebbles like drawing breath
percolators of
receding foam   the souls of
fishermen turned into seals
Lycados went all porpoise
Medon to skate   the boy sent
to Naxos   legs to coral
Aphrodite's cute boy-talk
her kiss as a seasonal

wind in the Cyclades gone

      and we're talking "real
gone" when we say 'gone'. Real, gone.
Get to. Beach your ship.
As the wind left behind in
the trees are these voices. Here.

*   *   *

and the voices say:

   'and ladies under-
garments are the bellweather
of the econo-
my.' And 'The Brotherhood of
the Faithless have advanced as
far as Jericho.'
As the wind in these beeches
and what's left behind
– these voices. 'His boob job has
made slimline knitwear a must.'

   'I drew my *iPad*
as I couldn't afford to
recharge it.' Get to.
Beach that thought. Make a light raft
then name it   the *Aphinar*

*   *   *

Hai-Far's Song

   and I ate bitterleaf
its tiny, serrated edge
in order that the
world seemed less bitter itself.
You gave me a name – Hai-Far –
and stripped me down to
the almond-white, and talked for
me. I felt like an
unshot bow, taut and cradled.
I thought of sorrel horses

   in the late season.
On the high eastern wall where
the radish withers
I gathered mulberries, once.
I never raised my apron.

*   *   *

the Green Man and not
Ronald Johnson's second tome
the original
where I took Hai-Far
so as to inhale her hair
eyes   constellations
tank top and   one bub
order a knife fight
but knife fights were off   just crisps
kitsch mercurial optics

Loughborough Junction
flaming but still a lock-in
an established fact –
as absinthe slips down a drain
allotments grow more quickly

Buckminster Fuller
dismissed *pi* from mathematics
read accordingly
Municipal islands 'all
Klimpt with violets'. Unquote.
Saplings and tubers
mutually parasitic.
'Got a lighter, mate?' Seedpods
for eyes. Spring in the gutters
crocus yellow livery

the pavement is mist,
Hai-Far sways, holds out her palm
'You are the Green Man
my liege, take these and seethe.' Primed,
I wade ash to the jukebox.

*   *   *

nightingale floorboards

if you will, tip-toe
fore-hearing the creak or crick
that is your own tense joints
and not their shy artistry —
the thoughts sprung rhythms betray.
Hai-Far sleeps behind a will-
ow trellis, spent.
You see a corncrake
taxi to a placid lake,
hear trees sing at a toe-tap.

you tinker with a tanka
every bit of you on points
gauge tautness or slack
as if one step were a full
mile. You oil your knees and start.

*   *   *

everybody is
here, wet, at The Takeaway —
hard hats and homeboys
slanting sleet has pushed us in
a troop of strolling players.
Crackle of fryers.
'Can you cut the black skin off?'
Crackle of fryers.
'Can you cut the black skin off?'
That hood, those shades, that swagger.

salt cellars jigger.
'Vinegar, my friend?' 'Or salt?'
Yesterday's papers.
The fryers. An old man's cough
from under seven layers.

'thighs, just thighs' says Gus
'That one and, er, that one. There.'
Her mouth to mobile.
'Wings? Not thighs, man. Wait, it's wings.'
'Make your mind up, girl!' Gus says.
Crackle of fryers.
'Can you cut the black skin off?'
A lull. Pickled eggs.
Day-Glo A2 poster peeled
corner *Blu Tack* blob. 'No, thighs!'

'two hake, three chips, please.'
'Can you cut the black skin off?'
'Yea, no black bits, man.'
Blue eyelashes blink. Blue bling.
Cerulean. Pure sky-stuff.

*   *   *

the Emperor T'ang
and Old Ez in the bathtub.
'Pass the loofer, Ez' says T'ang,
Ez does. The Emperor farts.
Their navels downloading hair.
'That "cedar" is from
Thrones, that "silkworm" from Cathay,
maybe the "kingfish-
er" is faux Olson, but that
"mulberry" is *Cathay*, sure.'

A high imperial pong.

Ha! Ha! MAKE IT NEW
Their merged dirt blocks the plughole.
Hai-Far brings fish and
chips. 'Vinegar, Emperor?
Vinegar, Ez?' Bubbles rise.

Ez: 'Any chance of a fig?'

*   *   *

53

the fishermen strain
together to haul in the
bell–buoys, this hammock
made of broken nets
is slung between   air and   air
diamonds of air–weave
held fast by taut tackle blocks
gull's cries?   or children's
such verisimilitude
to everything that is freed

   sky like *Tuinal*
tremor of the basking shark
sleep is a thick book
binding blue   the shallows clear
the deep   trawlerman's turquoise

*   *   *

'Who's Cathy?' says Gus. 'She fit?'

   'Buckminster Fuller
invented rhododendrons'
says the kingfisher
having fled its trembling branch.
'What about Colin?' it says,
'Or Gus?' and 'Is Colin Gus?'
One non sequitur
follows another.
Non sequiturs following
non sequiturs are not quite

   non sequiturs then?
'Follow that, my man.'
Kung will wait outside
breathing in iced mountain air.
He composes a canto.

where the voices say:
'I will be estranged from my
lover, not because
I no longer love her but
but because the word 'estranged'
is so beautiful.'
Say 'Under proscenium
arches, pear-shaped women are
vilified.' Say 'Self-doubt is
the new certainty.'

[Only five geese cross the sea]

  they say 'But this is
all *chinoiserie*, like Pound.'
And Kung will walk past
these bluey-green cedars, pluck-
ing a quatrefoil clover.

The Trap

I

    this avocado
sat plump on a chopping board
Sabatier knife
alongside   biding its time
that and a glazed onion
an advocate of
full lives lived on patios
purged opinion
sofas wrapped in cellophane
shagpile like *Dilaudid*

    this avocado
nine-banded armadillo
nosing greenery
armadillo's testicle
if the light is soft   *softly*

II

    see its scooped navel
tart with someone's slick *roulade*
please don't deny it
deny you took a sly bite
or swallowed one soaked half whole
so, The Advocate
Of Will went off to Soho
saw lanterns   slush   a
door-lit 'ho'   nicked a rickshaw
laden with avocados

    one fell off   bounced past
The Pagoda   one hell of
a sly, organic grenade
announced 'Please please reappraise
your petit bourgeoise malaise.'

III

   this avocado
in my humble opinion
a primed trap in a
white fridge   with *noblesse oblige*
take siege!   say the hungriest
the avocado
such an artful paradigm!
overdeveloped
lime in shot–dented armour
maim the green furlong of your

   tongue   one lolling here
sat plump on a chopping board
Sabatier knife
sharply marking time   along
with a bitter garlic bulb

The Glaziers

two men are manhandling an enormous sheet of glass across
a jostle of boulevards
at the exact moment the revolution starts,
the pane not smeared   with a X
– one forgot – so it might be seen.

Any airborne paving stone
– *for the struggle, for the people* – thrown
the length of the already body-strewn boulevard
or even the slightest movement, might cause it to smithereen.

Yet strangely, nothing seems more calm
nor less likely to agitate any *soixante-huitard*
than here beneath this filter-elm
where two men mime
holding a sheet of glass.

Line Lengths

supposedly last
to the edge of their fervor
as a cigarette
drawn to an orange end-stop
outside an empty airport
having foregone the
equinoctial crossing
reads now as nada
empty space   a new vista –
T.E. Hulme in Canada

land-haze and sea-haze
make a fine phosphorescent
gauze-porous border
every second immigrant
an Imagist   see
Madame Blavatsky
setting out Ouija board
in order to surf
the Internet of the Dead –
all moans strictly edited

a discarded roach
the runway is felt   seed pocked
fuzzy to touch   if
the lines come   they come measured
by all they cannot reach

The Nomads

I

always anticipate the
inevitable, forlorn
mishap, when the one blazing
buttercup in seventy
acres of shale is eaten
by a passing antelope.

II

suddenly, the flown
are tethered to hush,
blue, the colour of the known,
green–blue, the unknown
and beneath these, turquoise-brown,
kelp rustling the inner ear,
thrush in the stunt-fir by which they will set
up clapboard bathing huts for
all the Ladies of Vassar,
their calves white as halved shallots,
here, on the very shores of
the shores of Panthalassa,
[or, well, Watchtower Point] where a fresh wind
entices one Charles Olson, in his dented sou'wester
to haul in the horizon,
then the collapsed fishing shacks of Gloucester
– extract "Daimon" from "diamonds" –
as all dissolves at his ear
[and the only diamonds here the spaces defined
inside the net mesh.]
And this be his wish.

'One more endive, Guinevere?'
'Ho there – it's a porpoise.' [as
if gloss were the seal's purpose]

'There have been fresh air strikes on Syria.'
'Mr Melville is unwell.'

The revisions of time are severe.

III

off the coast of me...
raised beach / antimacassar;
us, speckles, decline,
mirage hiding mirage   we
abhor what we revere, to

travel is not to return.

Wake Up

(after Supervielle)

    surprisingly, the world dumped me; this rug, this well-thumbed novel,
you are going away;
our balcony is drifting off, a tiny white cloud
beyond the blinds.
One by one, each wall goes off
in a huff,
turning their backs on me, yacht sails
guided by sinuous undercurrent.

    The ceiling fan issues a seagull cry
like my pained, rotating heart.
The floorboards, keeping the lid

    on a secret, let out a groan,
as a man free-falling off a mist-covered mast
lightweight, dividing the air.

Spring Fever

I *The Sprung*

buffed up cylinders
Nitrous Oxide cylinders
by recycling bins
one flecked with sleet   one cinders
the young high as spring   [say the pollsters]   up all night
and then these   snowdrops
cold-eyed   tungsten   shaky
go fill all the skips   take up

gather in an apron these
little Barthesian spacecraft
the snowdrop's legal high so

these first flecks of sun   will lift
through the city's pollution
to tungsten clouds   tungsten sky

II *The Collapse*

my septum dissolved
smell of hydrangeas over-
rated   we only
miss what we remember   some
olfactory
the smell of your blouse
fresh spring fermenting within
like a child   that surge
of canal   its reek   its locks
merely spores in the sinus

O my days my days
I will snort up your chagrin
fill up the hole in my mind

between bolsters lain
on the barge of our shyness
we chalk up one white morning

And the Horse in Each Movement

I

if only the once
there is more sorrow
in the brim of a horse's
eyes than in your heart
distil a horse tear, keep it
in your hand and hold it there

II

if then your horse breathes
out, its breath is an ice-rose
exactly, though an
ice-rose that smells more of *Mace*,
the sorrow of its harness.

always, then, an ache
in the weary heart
also, though, a butt to kick
with your favoured right foot

so if the horse farts
it farts out edelweiss,
hay-waft, not syntax or sense;
the bud of this edelweiss,
the bud of this horse's arse
attract, repel, counterpoint
the past and then the present.
and this was no horse
but only the ice-breath of
something that has passed.

give me a moment

one fourth of your mind
ripened, three-fourths at impasse,
as stem-square leaves split for spring.
if no past nor present then
laziness is endeavour –
a sly horse or a windflower.

III
if somewhat unsure
of the entire history
of Chinese literature
– it has somehow passed you by –
then stoop to smell a windflower.

but a touch of wind
in the mare's swollen belly
two times four infolded hooves
will no way belie
this imminent double love –
the sawhorse of one frail foal
become the sawhorse
of two. How one prods an *iPad*,
nibbles on a sprig of thyme.
how one shucks a shoe.
This heart will never becalm.

give me a moment

if only the once
there is more mad joy
in the brim of a horse's
eyes than in your heart,
hear a horse-whinny, cup it
to your ear and hold it there

The Weight

if George Stubbs shouldered a dead stallion
up a staircase to hang it with blocks and pulleys
– mane like a parted waterfall, the great, sweating carcass –
merely in order to *see*
surely we can bear this weight upon us
more affliction than duty
the blood, guts, arteries, sweat and pus
of what this little art is

    in the meadow where the mare still goes down
        for the stallion;
in the meadow where the stallion goes down for the stallion
and the mare goes down

    for the mare; and in that meadow, couch grass, coleus and
        sphagnum moss;
then replicated in trillions
star–docked cinquefoil. And under that, soil.

The Waterfall

I

think of those old tales
where some live behind water-
falls, iced, formidable ply
of post-glacial onrush
as permanent backdrop   which
might make for monotony
a vertical sea   fluted sheer-sided as your mother's fridge
from inside the door   shrunk to a water droplet
no noise / white noise in your ear
– glockenspiel, melodeon –
inner night full-on gush and
then think about me –

outside of those cataracts
slanted against the outcrop
scant purchase on this fine – albeit fraying – fern
tethered just above
the dizzying drop,
craning manfully
but too scared to hear
what is gathered from these facts
    [eavesdroppers outmanoeuvred
    as everyone yearns to be
    overheard]   decide
the river below a piece
of lint, dropped, rending, a leaf.

II

I'm on a landing –
your gone pile in Forest Hill
wondering if I
should part the bamboo curtain
[in lieu of a door]
the inner sanctum, for a
brief word with your skeleton.

Basilisk

(from the Czech of Ferda Mravenec)

I

    and you, Basilisk
mere stain upon the wall,
a lozenge of will
waiting for a wild risk
to become available
without a green frisk
or flinch. Everything is stalled
inside that skull,
secretive as asterisks
studding a text, or braille

    the seeing can't trace.
You guard the grave-goods
of some long-slain king

    in a pyramid of ice,
eyes behind their hoods,
shut-in, but still all-seeing.

II

    and so, Basilisk
your tail-prints across this scroll
act as counterfoil.
Under your lime-green face-mask,
that your beautiful
exoskeletal husk
should remain still. Too still,
hid behind cutleaf,
too proud for an odalisque,
you need to frolic, then fall

into new looseness.
Once scrubbed and buttered
and wet from your showering

I will break this truce,
desecrate your quietude,
kiss you whilst you are peeing.

Meadow Saffrons

(after Apollinaire)

    supposedly this meadow is 'pretty', whatever pretty is,
though poisonous this time of year,
what with the cows not so much grazing here
as being slowly poisoned by meadow saffrons,
lilac colour, then shadow colour
under the eyes, grow or flower under the eyes
mauve as shadows, mauve as the curse
where I poison my entire life for one glimpse of your eyes.

    the school run in reverse
      – visibility jackets, loom bands, satchels, klaxons –
they pick crocuses which are like mothers, like mothers and
daughters lending each other eyeshadow

    until their lids ache, petals in the wind. Yet any cowherd can
coo softly enough to show
these shy, slow-moving cows, lowing with abandon,
out of this meadow with its half-chewed, poisonous flowers.

Slow Blow Job

I

as in that instant
of any sunset, sea change
of pale tangerine
to blood-orange, not looked for,
found, which is both high vision
and cool inner warmth
that taints the taut pine,
incline of serrated firs,
standard issue telescope
pulled out and up to the eyes,

the air rarefied,
some balmy low tide   fohn-topped
suffuses, yes, suffuses
everything, here, beyond
one warm glow-worm under glass.

II

no peyote bud
so nullifies the body
as lids brushed turquoise
as the skies over Roswell,
yes, Roswell, New Mexico
where researchers blow
into six weather balloons,
release them to air,
crackle of Geiger counters,
full orange protection suits

data collection.
Psychics. Trauma. ECT.
Old Bill and Arthur C Clarke,
the crop circle of your crown,
this whole thought held at waist-height.

III

   squat a pyramid
some Gothic roof-scape
whose tip takes the sun
live inside its pulsing ohm
where bellboys are glockenspiels
in each numbered room,
red plush and stud-buttons strain,
~~hookers on every floor~~   *Hoovers* on every floor,
pulleys of the dumb waiter,
sound going up and   sideways.

   hotels are spaceships,
fly, observe from underneath,
vast undercarriage
become a tilted sky, fly
synth swoosh sounds of   hand dyers.

IV

   he sees the Others
with strict regularity,
outlines, no outlines,
they have no outlines, just heat,
theophany, aftermath
bleached skies. Iron Range.
Their aerial surveillance.
Absentmindedly
tuck a stray hair behind an
ear, sound will be turned down, off.

   the world on its knees
has hereby invented me
through speech, am its speech-
bubble, lungs cryogenic.
Time stalls, moon replaces sun

V

sunlight's taut angles
peel-pull a tall building down
to stone gold basements,
bird shadow against flat sides,
brush of an eyelash
we are delivered
into Egypt, galley slaves
where truth is a feint whisper
or lift hydraulics shushing
into packed lobbies.

yes, submission, no.
I see the century turn,
not subservience
but gift and full up with love,
animal, no one breathing.

The Truce

(after Skřivánci na niti)

    my ceremonial sword will stay in its scabbard
its blade not yet whetted,
my young Gypsy bride
will sleep on top of the cupboard

    the duck feather double bed
too much of a comfort.
Or else she will run through the rooms trying light
after light

    after light, laughing. Yet we will see morning together, side
by side, there on the floorboards.

Dear Directeur

    I am in Aden
well   Aden or Harar   or
the Latin Quarter
one leg a mast   one leg wind
Marseille, maybe?   Marrakesh
whatever   not in these lines
one tusk, two tusks   five

    ~~scrape the blue sky and~~
~~hear its high curvature clang~~

    load-bearing weight   freak doldrums
O our sickly guild!
what whiteness glows in the hold
what black   *my dear Directeur*
coffee beans   guns   *move to trash*
————————— ~~*Malherbe*~~
~~Malheureux~~

    commission me a
clipper ship   commission me
a seven-masted schooner   seamless Barthian spacecraft
named the *Aphinar*   or   or
bound for Aphinar where the
trees are broccoli florets

    what once was my knee
is now air   air   and spreading
sunrise   we sail out of here

My Beautiful Comrade from the North

    supposedly still
arrives   wrapped in thrift store fur
an amber necklace
setting off the oval face
    her voice low as a cello

    a cello that plays
Dvorak's cello concerto
opening up Allegro
B minor then   B major
    nary a nod nor hello

    back by the Elvet
below that grey shrugging bridge
and greyer river
defined by its own stale glow
    goes over a pond weed weir

    sheet music you scan
left / right   and down then   left / right
in the Western tradition
some yawning a.m. when she
    dons her silk shift to prepare

    two coffees   blows through
the *Xpelair*   or tilts a
cherry *Actimel*   steps out of her bra
or bleaches her brown hair with
    lime like the Menaelicians

    the long-flanked Goddess
– Persephone, Demeter –
the other one   here
synonym and antonym
    of Muses   here   earplugs in

forgive   forgive me
I over elaborate   [that is my mandate]
two lost trainers hang
from lank festival hoardings
    the river   just a river

    just   the dour Elvet
chrome-brown eyes   brown half-top hat
lovely crooked teeth
so quiet inside   such sky
    the suitor is forced to say –

    'can I touch your hair?'
'No.' 'Can I touch your shoe?' 'No.'
'Can I touch your small
hard left breast?'   'No' and then   'No.'
    'Can I touch your furbelow?'

    'No.' 'Can I touch base?'
'No.' 'Is an outright, flat re-
    fusal your only tactic?'

    'No.'

[Prayer for] The Frazzled

pray it will always
vary, the yarn, as told by
the wild or wary
only an incidental
detail changing – sometimes a
car alarm, sometimes
an oriole sounding off
as your taxi pulls
into the neon blink-glint
of yule lights still in the trees

mid–February
under which the Creole girl
offers an obal
of sweet scent Lebanese Red
or smelted shoe sole

that fills your skull with
cinquefoil   septafoil   lint
as the whole yarn unravels